Janice VanCleave's
WILD, WACKY, and WEIRD
Science Experiments

Janice VanCleave's
Wild, Wacky, and Weird
PHYSICS
EXPERIMENTS

ROSEN
PUBLISHING

New York

This edition published in 2017 by:
The Rosen Publishing Group, Inc.
29 East 21st Street
New York, NY 10010

Library of Congress Cataloging-in-Publication Data

Names: VanCleave, Janice Pratt, author.
Title: Janice VanCleave's wild, wacky, and weird physics experiments / Janice
  VanCleave.
Other titles: Wild, wacky, and weird physics experiments
Description: New York, NY : Rosen Central, 2017. | Series: Janice
  VanCleave's wild, wacky, and weird science experiments | Includes
  bibliographical references and index. | Audience: 7-12.
Identifiers: LCCN 2016008914| ISBN 9781477789797 (library bound) |
  ISBN 9781477789773 (pbk.) | ISBN 9781477789780 (6-pack)
Subjects: LCSH: Physics--Experiments--Juvenile literature.
Classification: LCC QC25 .V255 2017 | DDC 530.078--dc23
LC record available at http://lccn.loc.gov/2016008914

Manufactured in China

Experiments first published in *Janice VanCleave's 202 Oozing, Bubbling, Dripping, and Bouncing Experiments* by John Wiley & Sons, Inc. copyright © 1996 Janice VanCleave.

CONTENTS

INTRODUCTION

Physics is the study of energy, matter, and forces and their relationship with each other. Physicists study everything from tiny atomic particles to the whole universe! Albert Einstein (1879–1955) is perhaps the most famous physicist, and many choose to follow in his footsteps.

The people who choose physics as a career do a variety of work. Some engineers investigate aircraft accidents and others work with nuclear power. Some physicists design high-speed trains, roller coasters, or lasers for surgery. All these people have something in common: They are constantly asking questions to learn even more about physics.

This book is a collection of science experiments about physics. How are electricity and magnetism related? How does a heavy ship float? How does gravity affect a siphon? You will find the answers to these and many other questions by doing the experiments in this book.

HOW TO USE THIS BOOK

Before you get started, be sure to read each experiment completely before starting. The following sections are included for all the experiments.

» **PURPOSE:** *The basic goals for the experiment.*

» **MATERIALS:** A list of supplies you will need.

You will experience less frustration and more fun if you gather all the necessary materials for the experiments before you begin. You lose your train of thought when you have to stop and search for supplies.

» **PROCEDURE:** *Step-by-step instructions on how to perform the experiment.*

Follow each step very carefully, never skip steps, and do not add your own. Safety is of the utmost importance, and by reading the experiment before starting, then following the instructions exactly, you can feel confident that no unexpected results will occur. Ask an adult to help you when you are working with anything sharp or hot. If adult supervision is required, it will be noted in the experiment.

» **RESULTS:** *An explanation stating exactly what is expected to happen.*

This is an immediate learning tool. If the expected results are achieved, you will know that you did the experiment correctly. If your results are not the same as described in the experiment, carefully read the instructions and start over from the first step.

» **WHY?** *An explanation of why the results were achieved.*

You will be rewarded with successful experiments if you read each experiment carefully, follow the steps in order, and do not substitute materials.

THE SCIENTIFIC METHOD

Scientists identify a problem or observe an event. Then they seek solutions or explanations through research and experimentation. By doing the experiments in this book, you will learn to follow experimental steps and make observations. You will also learn many scientific principles that have to do with physics.

In the process, the things you see or learn may lead you to new questions. For example, perhaps you have completed the experiment that determines whether magnetic forces act through paper. Now you wonder what would happen if you conducted the experiment with materials other than paper. That's great! All scientists are curious and ask new questions about what they learn. When you design a new experiment, it is a good idea to follow the scientific method.

1. Ask a question.

2. Do some research about your question. What do you already know?

3. Come up with a hypothesis, or a possible answer to your question.

4. Design an experiment to test your hypothesis. Make sure the experiment is repeatable.

5. Collect the data and make observations.

6. Analyze your results.

7. Reach a conclusion. Did your results support your hypothesis?

Many times the experiment leads to more questions and a new experiment.

Always remember that when devising your own science experiment, have a knowledgeable adult review it with you before trying it out. Ask them to supervise it as well.

FLASHLIGHT

PURPOSE To determine how a flashlight works.

MATERIALS flashlight that holds 2 size D batteries and has a remov-
able incandescent bulb
16-inch (40-cm) aluminum foil strip
duct tape
2 size D batteries

PROCEDURE

1. Unscrew the top section (which holds the bulb) from the flashlight.

2. Wrap one end of the foil strip around the base of the bulb holder.

3. Tape the two batteries together with the positive terminal of one touching the negative terminal of the other.

4. Stand the flat, negative terminal of the battery column on the free end of the foil strip.

5. Press the metal tip at the bottom of the flashlight bulb against the positive terminal of the battery, as shown in the diagram.

RESULTS The light glows.

WHY? The bulb glows when an electric current (flow of electric charges) flows through the circuit, which includes the battery, foil strip, and fine wire filament inside the flashlight bulb. The movement of the current through the wire filament causes the wire to get hot enough to give off light.

ATTRACTERS

PURPOSE To demonstrate the attraction between unlike charges.

MATERIALS two 9-inch (23-cm) round balloons
marking pen
two 1-yard (1-m) pieces of thread
masking tape
clean, dry, oil-free hair

PROCEDURE

NOTE: *This experiment works best on a cool, dry day.*

1. Inflate both balloons and tie their ends. Use the marking pen to label one balloon A and the other balloon B.

2. Tie one thread to the end of each balloon.

3. Tape the free ends of the threads to the top of a door frame so that the balloons hang about 8 inches (20 cm) apart.

4. Stroke balloon A on your hair about 10 times, then gently release it.

NOTE: *Leave the balloons hanging for the next experiment, Repellers.*

RESULTS The two balloons move toward each other and stick together.

WHY? All matter is made up of atoms, which have negatively charged electrons spinning around a positive nucleus. Electrons are rubbed off the hair and collect on balloon A; thus, the balloon becomes negatively charged. Since like charges repel (push away) each other, these nega-tive charges on balloon A repel the electrons of balloon B, causing B's surface to be more positively charged. The balloons now have opposite charges, so they are attracted to each other.

REPELLERS

PURPOSE To demonstrate the repulsion between like charges.

MATERIALS hanging balloons from previous experiment, Attracters
clean, dry, oil-free hair
helper

PROCEDURE

NOTE: *This experiment works best on a cool, dry day.*

1. Stroke balloon A on your hair 10 times.

2. Hold your balloon as your helper rubs balloon B on your hair 10 times.

3. Gently release the balloons.

RESULTS The balloons move away from each other.

WHY? Rubbing both balloons on your hair results in a buildup of negatively charged electrons on their surfaces. The balloons move away from each other because they have the same charge and like charges repel.

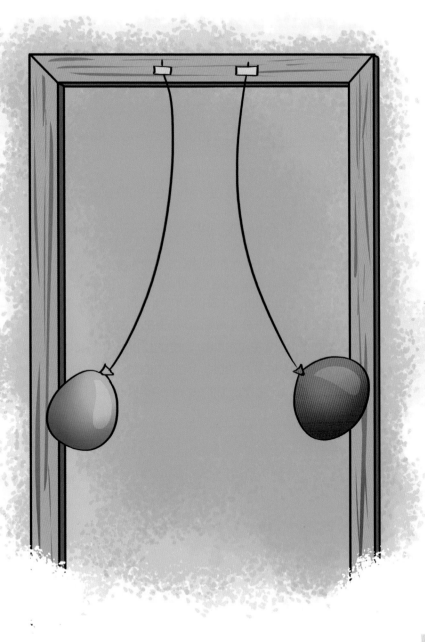

Repellers

STICKY?

PURPOSE To demonstrate the effect of static electricity.

MATERIALS transparent tape

PROCEDURE

1. Press two pieces of tape onto a table, leaving a small piece hanging over the edge.

2. Hold the ends of the tape and quickly pull both pieces up off the table.

3. Bring the two pieces near each other, but not touching.

RESULTS The pieces of tape move away from each other.

WHY? When there is a buildup of static charges (stationary electrical charges) in one place, the object is said to have static electricity. Pulling the tape pieces from the table causes them to pick up negatively charged electrons from the atoms in the table. Both pieces of tape are negatively charged. Materials with like charges repel each other.

Sticky?

Line Up

PURPOSE To demonstrate how electricity and magnetism are related.

MATERIALS long iron nail
piece of cardboard, 6 inches (15 cm) square
1 yard (1 m) 18-gauge insulated wire
roll of masking tape
6-volt battery
iron filings (purchase at a teacher-supply store)
adult helper

PROCEDURE

1. Ask an adult to use the nail to punch a hole through the center of the cardboard.

2. Wrap the wire tightly around the nail, leaving about 6 inches (15 cm) of free wire on each end.

3. Ask your helper to strip the insulation off both ends of the wire and to insert the wire-wrapped nail through the hole in the cardboard.

4. Make the cardboard sit flat by placing it on the roll of tape. Then attach one end of the wire to either battery terminal.

5. Sprinkle a thin layer of iron filings on the cardboard around the coiled wire.

6. Attach the free wire to the open battery terminal.

7. Observe the pattern made by the iron filings.

CAUTION: *The nail and wires will get hot if left connected to the battery. Be sure to interrupt the circuit by disconnecting one wire from one pole.*

RESULTS The iron filings form a starburst pattern around the coil of wire.

WHY? There is a magnetic field around all wires carrying an electric current. The iron filings are pulled toward the magnetized nail and form a starburst pattern around the coil of wire.

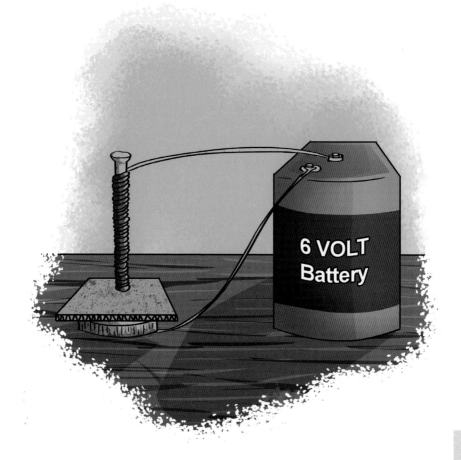

STICKERS

PURPOSE To discover what materials are attracted to a magnet.

MATERIALS testing materials: aluminum foil, copper wire, glass marble, iron nail, paper, steel BBs, wooden match
bar magnet

PROCEDURE

1. Lay the testing materials on a wooden table.

2. Touch the magnet to, and slowly move the magnet away from, each material.

3. Observe and record which materials cling to the magnet.

RESULTS The iron nail and the BBs are the only materials that cling to the magnet.

WHY? One end of a magnet called its north pole is attracted to the earth's magnetic north pole. The other end of the magnet is attracted to the earth's magnetic south pole. All magnetic materials have clusters of atoms that like a magnet are dipolar (have both a north and a south pole). These clusters are called domains. In magnetic materials, many of the domains line up with their north poles pointing in the same direction. The more uniform the arrangement of domains, the stronger the magnetic property of the material. Nonmagnetic materials do not have domains.

More Muscle

PURPOSE To determine what part of a magnet has the strongest attracting ability.

MATERIALS scissors
ruler
string
bar magnet
masking tape
box of about 100 small paper clips
large bowl

PROCEDURE

1. Cut two 3-foot (1-m) pieces of string.

2. Tie one end of each string to each end of the magnet.

3. Tape the free ends of the strings to the top of a door frame.

4. Adjust the length of the strings so that the magnet hangs in a level position and is at a height that is easy for you to reach.

5. Spread the paper clips in the bottom of the bowl.

6. Raise the bowl so that the magnet touches the paper clips.

7. Slowly lower the bowl.

8. Observe where the clips cling to the magnet.

RESULTS Most of the clinging paper clips are near the ends of the magnet.

WHY? All magnets are surrounded by an area called a magnetic field. This area is made of invisible lines of force coming out of the north pole of the magnet, around each side, and into the south pole of the magnet. The magnetic force lines are closest together at the poles, which gives the poles the strongest magnetic attraction.

Straight Through

PURPOSE To determine if magnetic forces act through paper.

MATERIALS sheet of printer paper
bar magnet
thumbtack

PROCEDURE

1. Lay the sheet of paper on a wooden table.

2. Place the magnet so that its north pole is under the edge of the paper.

3. Position the thumbtack on top of the paper where the paper covers the end of the magnet.

4. Hold the uncovered end of the magnet with your hand and move the magnet from side to side under the paper.

RESULTS The paper is not attracted to the magnet, but the thumbtack is. Moving the magnet caused the thumbtack to move.

WHY? Around every magnet is an invisible magnetic field. Some materials, such as paper, do not stop or disrupt the pattern of the force field. Materials that allow lines of magnetic force to pass through without any disruptions in the magnetic field are said to be nonpermeable. Nonpermeable materials are not attracted to a magnet. The lines of magnetic force pass through the paper with no change in their direction; thus, the paper is nonpermeable and nonmagnetic.

Straight Through

FLOATING BOAT

PURPOSE To determine how a heavy ship floats.

MATERIALS scissors
20 paper clips
ruler

small bucket
aluminum foil
tap water

PROCEDURE

1. Cut two 12-inch (30-cm) squares from the aluminum foil.

2. Wrap one of the metal squares around 10 paper clips and squeeze the foil into a tight ball.

3. Fold the four edges of the second aluminum square up to make a small boat.

4. Place 10 paper clips in the boat.

5. Fill the bucket with water.

6. Set the boat on the water's surface in the bucket.

7. Place the metal ball on the water's surface.

RESULTS The boat floats and the ball sinks.

WHY? The ball and boat both have the same weight, but the ball takes up a smaller space than does the boat. The amount of water pushed aside by an object equals the force of water pushing upward on the object. The larger boat pushes more water out of its way than does the ball and thus there is enough upward force to cause it to float. Ships are very heavy, but they are large, which increases their buoyancy.

Floating Boat

Bubbler

PURPOSE To determine what happens to air bubbles in water.

MATERIALS 1-gallon (4-liter) large-mouthed jar
           tap water
           flexible drinking straw
           small balloon

PROCEDURE

1. Fill the jar with water.

2. Place one end of the straw in the water at the bottom of the jar.

3. Inflate the balloon and twist the neck to prevent the air from escaping.

4. Slip the mouth of the balloon over the end of the straw. Hold securely with your fingers.

5. Untwist the balloon and allow the air to escape slowly through the straw.

6. Watch the end of the straw in the water and notice the movement of the air as it exits the tube.

RESULTS Bubbles are formed at the end of the straw. The bubbles rise to the top of the water's surface and escape into the air.

WHY? The air bubbles push water out of their way as they emerge from the end of the straw. The weight of the water pushed aside equals the amount of upward force on the bubbles. This force is called buoyancy. The air bubbles are so light that they quickly push to the top of the water where they break through the water's surface and mix with the air surrounding the jar.

HANGING BUBBLES

PURPOSE To discover how gravity affects the shape of soap bubbles.

MATERIALS small bowl
¼ cup (60 ml) dishwashing liquid
¼ cup (60 ml) water
1 teaspoon (5 ml) sugar
spoon
large empty thread spool

PROCEDURE

1. Place the bowl on a table outdoors. Add the dishwashing liquid, water, and sugar to the bowl.

2. Dip one end of the spool into the mixture.

3. Place your mouth against the dry end of the spool, and gently blow through the hole in the spool.

4. Blow a large bubble, but do not allow it to break free from the spool. Then, place your finger over the hole you blew through to prevent the air from leaking out of the soap bubble, as shown.

5. Study the bubble's shape.

RESULTS A bubble that is slightly pointed on the bottom hangs from the spool. Tiny, threadlike streams of liquid quickly swirl down the sides of the bubble and collect at the bottom, where they form drops and fall.

WHY? The molecules of dishwashing liquid and water link together to form a thin layer of elastic liquid that stretches to surround the air blown into it. Gravity pulls the spherical bubble downward, forming a slight point at the bottom. The molecules that make up the thin film of the bubble are also pulled downward, causing the bubble's skin to continue to become thinner at the top until it finally breaks.

Antigravity?

PURPOSE To demonstrate overcoming the forces of gravity.

MATERIALS modeling clay
baby food jar
tap water
red or blue food coloring
spoon
drinking straw

PROCEDURE

1. Press a marble-sized piece of clay against the inside of the bottom of the jar.

2. Fill the jar one-half full with water.

3. Add 3 or 4 drops of food coloring to the water and stir.

4. Slowly lower the straw into the colored water.

5. Push the bottom end of the straw into the clay. The straw can now stand in a vertical position.

6. Quickly turn the jar upside down over a sink.

7. Turn the jar right side up and set it on a table.

8. Observe the contents of the straw.

RESULTS Colored water remains in the straw. The height of the water in the straw is the same as that of the water before it was poured out.

WHY? Water molecules are attracted to each other. At the surface of the water, the molecules tug on each other so much that a skinlike surface is produced. The air in the straw pushes up on the water when the jar is inverted and water molecules are pulling from side to side. These forces are greater than the downward force of gravity; thus, the water remains in the straw.

Up and Over

PURPOSE To determine what a siphon is and how gravity affects it.

MATERIALS 2 drinking glasses
tap water
flexible drinking straw

PROCEDURE

1. Fill one glass with water.

2. Bend the straw and place the short end in the glass of water.

3. Suck on the free end of the straw with your mouth until water comes out.

4. Quickly put the end of the straw into the empty glass.

RESULTS The water flows in a steady stream up the straw then down from the higher glass to the lower glass.

WHY? A siphon allows liquids to flow uphill. It is a device that lifts a liquid up and over the edge of one container and into another container at a lower level. To start the siphoning process, the tube must be filled with water. One way to do this is by sucking the air out of the tube. Air pressure is the result of gravity pulling gas molecules in the air downward. In the open glass, the air pressure outside the straw pushing down on the surface of the water is great enough to force the liquid up as high as the bend in the straw. Gravity then pulls the water down and out of the straw. Every drop of water that flows out of the straw leaves an empty space inside the straw. Water from the glass is pushed into the straw to fill this space. As long as the upper end of the straw remains below the surface of the water, a steady stream of liquid flows out of the lower end of the straw.

FASTER

PURPOSE To demonstrate that heavier things fall faster than lighter things.

MATERIALS paper

book larger than the paper

PROCEDURE

1. Hold the paper in one hand and the book in the other, keeping both waist-high.

2. Drop the book and the paper at the same time.

3. Observe the paper and book as they fall and strike the floor.

RESULTS The book hits the floor before the paper does.

WHY? Gravity causes the speed of falling objects to increase at a rate of 32 feet per second (9.8 m per sec) for every second of falling time. All things would fall at this rate, regardless of their weight, in a vacuum. But air molecules in the earth's atmosphere push against falling objects and slow their falling rate. Heavier objects, such as the book, push through the air with more force than do lightweight objects, such as the paper. Thus, heavier objects fall through air faster than do lightweight objects.

Faster

TOGETHER

PURPOSE To demonstrate that gravity pulls all things down at the same rate.

MATERIALS paper

book larger than the paper

PROCEDURE

1. Place the paper on top of the book. Do not have any of the paper hanging over the edges of the book.

2. Hold the book waist-high and drop it.

3. Observe the paper and book as they fall and strike the floor.

RESULTS The book and the paper fall together.

WHY? Because gravity pulls equally on all objects, the lighter paper and the heavier book both fall at the same rate when air resistance is removed. The previous experiment, Faster, showed that the lightweight paper was slowed by the air, while the heavy book was hardly slowed at all. In this experiment, however, the air molecules did not press against the paper because it was on top of the book. So the book and the paper fell at the same rate, just as they would if they were dropped in a vacuum.

STRAW BALANCE

PURPOSE To determine how the center of gravity affects a balance.

MATERIALS ruler
drinking straw
marking pen
scissors
small index card
straight pin
2 wooden blocks of equal height and not as wide as the
length of the straw
adult helper

PROCEDURE

1. Use the ruler to find the center of the straw and mark the spot with the marking pen.

2. Cut a 1-inch (2.5-cm) slit in the same place on each end of the straw, as shown in the diagram.

3. Cut the index card in half lengthwise and insert the card pieces in the slits in the straw.

4. Ask an adult to punch the straight pin through the center of the straw.

5. Position the two wooden blocks on a table and place the ends of the pin on the edges of the blocks.

6. Move the card pieces out and in until you find the positions that make the straw level with the table.

NOTE: *Save the straw balance for the next experiment, Creature Weigh-In.*

RESULTS Moving the card pieces causes the straw to drop and rise.

WHY? The farther a piece of card is moved away from the pin, the more downward the rotation of the straw on that side. The straw is balanced when the position of the cards places the center of gravity at the place where the pin is inserted.

CREATURE WEIGH-IN

PURPOSE To compare the weight of a paper creature with that of paper hole-punch circles.

MATERIALS pencil
index card
scissors
straw balance from previous experiment
paper hole-punch

PROCEDURE

1. Draw your version of a space creature on half of the index card.

2. Cut out the creature and place it on one of the balance's index cards.

3. Punch paper circles from the remaining portion of the index card and continue to place them on the empty card until the straw is level with the table.

RESULTS The end holding the paper creature falls down, but starts to rise as paper circles are added to the opposite card. Too many circles lift the creature above the balancing point.

WHY? The downward pull that gravity has on an object is called its weight. Placing the paper creature on one side of the balance increases the weight on that side. Adding paper circles to the opposite card begins to balance the weight of the creature. When the total weight of the paper circles equals the weight of the paper creature, the balance will be level with the table. The level balance indicates that the pull of gravity is the same on both sides of the balance.

Creature Weigh-In

BALANCING POINT

PURPOSE To locate an object's center of gravity.

MATERIALS scissors

manila folder

paper hole-punch

12-inch (30-cm) piece of string

washer

pushpin

pinboard

ruler

pen

PROCEDURE

1. Cut one side of the manila folder into an irregular shape.

2. Punch five randomly spaced holes in the edge of the paper with the paper hole-punch.

3. Tie one end of the string to the washer and the other end to the push-pin.

4. Stick the pushpin through one of the holes in the paper and into the pinboard.

5. Allow the paper and string to swing freely.

6. Use the ruler and pen to mark a line on the paper next to the string.

7. Move the pushpin to the other holes and mark the position of the hanging string each time. Do this for the remaining four holes.

8. Place the paper on the end of your index finger. Your finger is to be below the point where the lines cross.

RESULTS The paper balances on your finger.

WHY? Center of gravity is the balancing point of an object. The center of gravity of the paper is the point where the five lines cross. Hold your finger under that point and observe the balance.

HEAVY AIR

PURPOSE To demonstrate that air has weight.

MATERIALS modeling clay
pencil
four 12-inch (30-cm) pieces of string
yardstick (meterstick)
three 9-inch (23-cm) balloons (must all be the same size)

PROCEDURE

1. Use the clay to secure the end of the pencil to the edge of a table.

2. Suspend the measuring stick by tying one of the strings to the center of the stick and looping the free ends around the pencil. Adjust the position of the string in order to balance the measuring stick.

3. Use 2 strings to suspend 2 uninflated balloons an equal distance from the center support string. Move the balloons back and forth until the stick and the balloons balance.

4. Inflate a balloon and attach the remaining string. Make a loop with the string ends.

5. Remove one of the uninflated balloons and replace it in exactly the same position with the inflated balloon.

RESULTS The uninflated balloons make the stick balance, but the inflated balloon makes the stick unbalanced.

WHY? The stick balances when the downward pull is the same on both sides of the center support string. Replacing the uninflated balloon with an inflated balloon puts extra weight on one side of the stick. The weight of the air inside the inflated balloon increases the downward pull on the stick, causing it to move down on that side.

Belted

PURPOSE To make a model of belted wheels.

MATERIALS hammer
large 8-penny nail
2 metal jar lids of equal size
wooden board, 2 by 4 by 12 inches (5 by 10 by 30 cm)
ruler
2 small 6-penny nails
rubber band
marking pen
adult helper

PROCEDURE

1. Ask an adult to use the hammer and nail to make a hole in the center of each lid.

2. Ask your adult helper to attach the lids to the board with the nails, as shown, leaving enough space between the lids and the heads of the nails so that the lids turn easily.

3. Connect the two lids by stretching the rubber band around the outer rims of both lids.

4. Use the marking pen to mark lines on the tops of the lids directly across from each other.

5. Use your hand to turn one lid clockwise so that it makes one complete turn. Observe the marks.

RESULTS Both lids turn clockwise, and the marks return to their original positions at the same time.

WHY? The lids and the rubber band act as belted wheels. A belt allows one rotating wheel to turn another distant wheel. Wheels connected by a belt rotate in the same direction. Connected wheels of equal circumference (the distance around the outside of a circle) turn at the same speed.

FLAG RAISER

PURPOSE To determine what a fixed pulley is, and how it makes work easier.

MATERIALS pencil (must be small enough to slide through the hole in the thread spool}
large, empty thread spool
6-foot (2-m) piece of string
blue and red crayons
index card
masking tape
helper

PROCEDURE

1. Place the pencil through the hole in the spool. The spool must turn easily on the pencil.

2. Tie the ends of the string together.

3. Draw and color a flag on the index card.

4. Tape the side with the flag to the string.

5. Place the loop of string over the spool, with the flag hanging at the bottom of the loop.

6. Ask your helper to hold the ends of the pencil, one in each hand at arm's length over his or her head.

7. Pull down on the string opposite the flag.

8. Observe the distance the string is pulled down and the distance and direction the flag moves.

RESULTS The length of string pulled down over the spool equals the distance the flag moves upward.

WHY? A pulley is a simple machine that consists of a wheel, usually grooved, that holds a cord. A fixed pulley stays in place; the pulley turns as the cord moves over the wheel, and a load is raised as the cord is pulled. The spool is a fixed pulley that allows you to pull down on the string and raise the flag upward. Placing a fixed pulley at the top of a tall flag-pole makes the job of raising a flag easier than if you had to carry the flag up the pole. A fixed pulley makes work easier by changing the direction of the effort force (the push or pull needed to move an object).

THREADS

PURPOSE To determine how a screw is like an inclined plane.

MATERIALS pencil
ruler
sheet of printer paper
scissors
marking pen
transparent tape

PROCEDURE

1. Draw a right triangle with a base 014 inches (10 cm) and a height of 6 inches (15 cm} on the paper.

2. Cut out the triangle.

3. Color the diagonal edge of the paper triangle with the marking pen.

4. Tape the triangle to the pencil with the colored edge facing up, as shown in the diagram.

5. Rotate the pencil to wrap the paper tightly around the pencil.

6. Tape the end of the wrapped paper to itself.

7. Count the number of diagonal stripes made by the colored edge of the triangle that is wrapped around the pencil.

RESULTS There are diagonal bands spiraling around the pencil.

WHY? A screw is an inclined plane (a sloping or slanting surface) that is wrapped around a cylinder to form spiraling ridges. Screws look like spiral staircases. A common example of a screw is a wood screw. As this screw rotates, it moves into the wood a certain distance. This distance depends on the screw's pitch (the distance between the ridges winding around the screw). Each colored band on the paper around the pencil represents a spiral ridge on a screw, which is called a thread. Screws with a shorter distance between the threads are easier to tum.

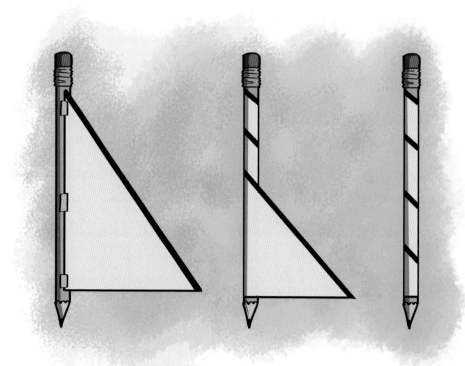

OPENER

PURPOSE To determine what a wedge is and how it helps you to do work.

MATERIALS
pencil
ruler
thick cardboard

scissors
small book

PROCEDURE

1. Draw a right triangle with a base of 4 inches (10 cm) and a height of 2 inches (5 cm) on the cardboard.

2. Cut out the triangle.

3. Place the book on a table.

4. Hold the triangle in your hand, with the 4-inch (10-cm) base against the table and the 2-inch (5-cm) side upright.

5. Support the book so that it does not move forward as you gently push the cardboard triangle under one edge of the book.

6. Observe the direction of motion of both the cardboard triangle and the book.

RESULTS The cardboard triangle moves forward and the book rises upward.

WHY? A wedge is a simple machine shaped like an inclined plane. A wedge is actually more like a moving inclined plane. Instead of objects being pushed up its inclined side, the plane moves forward, raising the object. The effort force always pushes the wedge forward, and the load (the object being moved) moves to the side (perpendicular to the direction of the effort force). The tapered edge of the triangle, like all wedges, enters and makes a path for the larger part of the wedge that follows. Once an opening is made by the point of the wedge, materials are easily pried apart by the gradually widening body of the wedge. It takes less effort to move an object using a wedge than it takes to move it with only your hands.

LEVERS

PURPOSE To demonstrate the effectiveness of a lever.

MATERIALS 4 books

2 pencils

PROCEDURE

1. Stack the books on a table.

2. Put your little finger under the edge of the bottom book in the stack and try to lift the books.

3. Place one pencil under the edge of the bottom book in the stack.

4. Place the second pencil under the first pencil near the book.

5. Push down on the end of the second pencil with your little finger and try to lift the books.

RESULTS It is very difficult to lift the books with your finger alone, but easy when two pencils are used.

WHY? The pencils form a lever (a rigid bar that rotates around a fixed point). One of the pencils acts as a fulcrum (a point of rotation) for the second pencil. As the distance from where you push down to the fulcrum increases, the easier it is to lift the load on the opposite end. Levers are simple machines that multiply the force that you apply. This makes moving or lifting large objects easier.

GLOSSARY

ATOMS The smallest building blocks of matter.

BUOYANCY The upward force exerted by a liquid such as water on any object in or on the liquid.

CENTER OF GRAVITY Point at which an object balances.

CIRCUMFERENCE The distance around the outside of a circle.

DOMAIN A cluster of atoms with their north poles pointing in the same direction.

EFFORT FORCE The push or pull needed to move an object.

ELECTRIC CURRENT Flow of electric charges.

ELECTRONS The negatively charged particle in an atom.

FULCRUM The fixed point of rotation on a lever.

INCLINED PLANE A slanting or sloping surface used to raise an object to a higher level.

LOAD Object being moved.

MAGNETIC FIELD Area around a magnet in which the force of the magnet affects the movement of other magnetic objects; made up of invisible lines of magnetic force.

MAGNETIC NORTH POLE Point on the earth that attracts the north pole of magnets.

MAGNETIC SOUTH POLE Point on the earth that attracts the south pole of magnets.

MATTER Any substance that takes up space and has weight.

MOLECULE The smallest particle of a substance; made of one or more atoms.

NUCLEUS The central part of an atom.

REPEL To push away.

ROTATE To spin on one's axis.

SIMPLE MACHINE A lever, inclined plane, wheel and axle, screw, wedge, or pulley.

SIPHON A device that lifts a liquid up and over the edge of one container and into another container at a lower level.

SPHERICAL Shaped like a ball.

VACUUM Space with nothing in it.

WEIGHT The downward pull that gravity has on an object.

FOR MORE INFORMATION

American Physics Society
  1 Physics Ellipse
  College Park, MD 20740
  (301) 209.3200
  website: www.aps.org
  Solve a mystery by doing an experiment through PhysicsQuest, read This Month in
  Physics History, or learn about careers in physics.

Canadian Association of Physicists
  555 King Edward Avenue
  3rd Floor
  Ottawa, Ontario, Canada
  K1N 7N5
  (613) 562-5614
  website: www.cap.ca
  Find out about careers in physics, enter the Art of Physics photography contest, or
  learn about student scholarships and prizes.

Intel
  2200 Mission College Blvd.
  Santa Clara, CA 95054-1549
  (408) 765-8080
  website: http://www.intel.com
  Read student profiles of winning research projects from the Intel International Science
  and Engineering Fair, and find educational material about Women in Science, tips for
  your science fair project, and links to other competitions.

National Science Foundation (NSF)
  4201 Wilson Boulevard
  Arlington, Virginia 22230, USA
  (703) 292-5111
  website: http://www.nsf.gov/

The NSF is dedicated to science, engineering, and education. Learn how to be a Citizen Scientist, read about the latest scientific discoveries, and discover the newest innovations in technology.

The Society for Science and the Public
 Student Science
 1719 N Street, NW
 Washington, DC 20036
 (800) 552-4412
 website: https://student.societyforscience.org
 The Society for Science and the Public presents many science project resources, such as science news for students, the latest updates on the Intel Science Talent Search and the Intel International Science and Engineering Fair, and information about cool jobs and doing science.

USA Science & Engineering Festival
 Walter E. Washington Convention Center
 801 Mount Vernon Place NW
 Washington, D.C. 20001
 (202) 459-0880
 website: http://www.usasciencefestival.org
 The USA Science & Engineering Festival is a national grassroots effort to advance STEM education and inspire the next generation of scientists and engineers. Nationwide school programs, contests, and events year-round culminate in a two-day Grand Finale Expo, free of charge.

WEBSITES

Because of the changing nature of Internet links, Rosen Publishing has developed an online list of websites related to the subject of this book. This site is updated regularly. Please use this link to access this list:

http://www.rosenlinks.com/JVCW/physic

FOR FURTHER READING

Ardley, Neil. *101 Great Science Experiments*. New York: DK Ltd., 2014.

Ball, Nate. *The Science Unfair* (Alien in My Pocket). New York: Harper, 2014.

Biskup, Agnieszka. *Super Cool Forces and Motion Activities with Max Axiom* (Science and Engineering Activity). North Mankato, MN: Capstone Press, 2015.

Brown, Jordan. *Science Stunts: Fun Feats of Physics*. Watertown, MA: Charlesbridge Publishing, 2016.

Buczynski, Sandy. *Designing a Winning Science Fair Project* (Information Explorer Junior). Ann Arbor, MI: Cherry Lake Publishing, 2014.

Gardner, Robert. *The Physics of Sports Science Projects* (Exploring Hands-On Science Projects). Berkeley Heights, NJ: Enslow Publishers, Inc., 2013.

Henneberg, Susan. *Creating Science Fair Projects with Cool New Digital Tools* (Way Beyond PowerPoint: Making 21st Century Presentations). New York: Rosen Central, 2014.

Margles, Samantha. *Mythbusters Science Fair Book*. New York: Scholastic, 2011.

Mercer, Bobby. *Junk Drawer Physics: 50 Awesome Experiments That Don't Cost a Thing*. Chicago: Chicago Review Press, Inc., 2014.

Rompella Natalie. *Experiments in Light and Sound with Toys and Everyday Stuff* (Fun Science). North Mankato, MN: Capstone Press, 2016.

Ruff Ruffman's 44 Favorite Science Activities (Fetch! with Ruff Ruffman). Somerville MA: Candlewick Press, 2015.

Walton, Ruth. *Let's Go to the Playground* (Let's Find Out). Mankato, MN: Sea-to-Sea Publications, 2013.

INDEX

34, 36
and water column, 30–31, 32

I
inclined plane, 50–51, 52–53
iron filings, 16–17

L
lever, 54
lifting heavy objects, 54
load, 53

M
magnetic field, 17, 21, 22
magnetic force, 6, 21, 22
magnetic force lines, 21, 22
magnetism, 16–17, 18, 20–21, 22
magnets, 18, 20–21, 22
matter, 4, 10
molecules, 28–29

N
nonpermeable materials, 22
north pole, magnetic, 18, 21, 22
nucleus, 10

P
physics, definition, 4

R
repulsion, 10, 12, 14
rotation, 47

S
safety, 5
scientific method, 6–7
screw, 50–51
ships, 24
simple machines, 48–49, 50–51,
   52–53, 55
siphons, 32–33
soap bubbles, 28–29
south pole, magnetic, 18, 21
speed of falling objects, 34, 36
static electricity, 14

T
thread, screw, 51

V
vacuum, 34, 36